The Bear-Walker
and Other Stories

Basil H. Johnston

Illustrated by
David A. Johnson

RŎM
Royal Ontario Museum

© 1995 Royal Ontario Museum

First published in 1995 by the Royal Ontario Museum,
100 Queen's Park, Toronto, Ontario M5S 2C6

Managing Editor: Glen Ellis
Designer: Virginia Morin

Canadian Cataloguing in Publication Data
Johnston, Basil, 1929-
    The bear-walker and other stories
ISBN 0-88854-415-4

1. Ojibwa Indians - Folklore. 2. Indians of North
America - Folklore. I. Johnson, David, 1962-
II. Royal Ontario Museum. III. Title.

E99.C6J65 1995   398.2'089973   C95-931943-3

Printed and bound in Canada by Friesen Printers

Contents

The Bear-Walker *(Mukwo-bimossae)*

7

The Great Lynx *(Mishi-bizheu)*

17

Mer-Man *(Nebaunaubae)*

21

Fish *(Geegoohnuk)*

27

Red Willows *(Zeesigoobimeeshuk)*

33

The Snake and the Man *(Ginaebig, Ininih gayae)*

39

The Woodpecker *(Paupaussae)*

49

Bull Frog *(Taendae)*

55

Vision *(Waussaeyaubindumowin)*

61

Introduction

Anishinaubaek (singular, Anishinaubae) is an Ojibway word translating variously as "the good beings" and "from whence man descended." It is the name the Ojibway people prefer to call themselves. As yet, there is no standardized spelling, but the pronunciation is generally (a)nish-NAH-bek (singular [a]nish-NAH-bay).

These tales are told by Basil Johnston, Sam Ozawamik, and Frank Shawbedees—Anishinaubae members of the Cape Croker, the Wikwemikong, and the Saugeen First Nation respectively. The stories were collected and translated from the Anishinaubae by Basil Johnston.

The Bear-Walker

Mukwo-bimossae

Told by Frank Shawbedees

Collected and translated from the Anishinaubae
by Basil H. Johnston

One Anishinaubae wanted to learn what you might call medicine. Actually, he really wanted to learn all kinds of things. Besides, he wanted to understand himself.

This young man could not speak Anishinaubae. He had lost his language. (This is rather new.)

Oh, and by the way, this young Anishinaubae went to many different places seeking whatever it was that he was searching for. At that time he really didn't know.

Eventually, he heard that a medicine man lived in such-and-such a place. And so he went there and spoke to that man.

"I'm looking for something, but I really don't know what it is that I'm looking for. At the same time I want to know medicine, not bad medicine though. I want to help my fellow Anishinaubaek."

Ah! It was settled. "Very well! I'll try you," this man said.

Some call this person medicine man. Others call such a person many other terms in different places wherever I have gone. Some call him bear-walker. There are two kinds of bear-walkers—those who practice evil medicine and those who try to help their fellow Anishinaubaek.

"Very well! I'll teach you. But it will not be fast, rest assured," the bear-walker explained. Ahah! he already knows, though, what young people are like nowadays. They are anxious, they are by nature anxious. Why? Nobody knows. And, just like the others, this young man wanted to learn things in a great hurry.

Once they were about, walking around. They were looking into a river. "Tell me, do you see anything?" this medicine man asked.

"Not a thing," replied the young man. "What?"

"Oh, nothing about nothing," said the teacher.

On they went. The bear-walker looked here and there. "Do you see anything, Anishinaubae?"

"Nothing."

"That's fine. That's all for now."

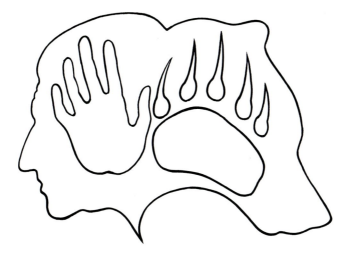

They went back to where they were living. They were sitting. "What are you thinking?" he inquired, this bear-walker.

"It's hard to believe how long you take! It's hard to believe how slow you are for me to learn anything! You are slow teaching me!"

The bear-walker spoke. "Today, I asked what you saw. Do you know what you told me?"

"Yes, of course. Nothing!"

"You're right . . . you're right. You didn't see anything."

"I don't understand," the young man answered.

"We went by the river. 'Do you see anything?' I asked you. 'Nothing,' you replied. You didn't see yourself in that water."

That was that.

Early the next morning, as the moon was setting, they once more went walking about, along the same way. The bear-walker looked about. "Ahah! Do you see that flower over there—in the middle of the pond?"

"Oh, there are a great many out there," replied the young man.

"Over there," said the bear-walker. "Over there! Alright, go get it!"

The young man set out at once, into the water. He went out only as far as his knees. "Is this the one you mean?"

"No. Further."

On he went once more. By now the water was up to here, up to his waist, where the belt goes. "Is this it?"

"No! That flower yonder."

He went out further. And the water too was getting more foul as he went out. That water wasn't flowing anywhere (even though a river was flowing nearby). It is ever still.

"Is this the one?"

"No, a little further on yet. There it is over there."

The Anishinaubae went on as he was instructed. (The water has already reached his neck.) "Is this it?"

"Yes, that's the one," answered the bear-walker.

The young man was just about to break off the stem.

"No! Don't! Don't!" he said. "Don't break it! I want the entire plant, what's underwater also!"

"Ah! It's impossible to satisfy this man!"

The Anishinaubae put his hand down below. He pulled and pulled. But it wouldn't give way, not even a little. "What should I do?" he yelled out. "What can I do?"

"You're the one who's there. Think what you should do," the bear-walker answered him.

He didn't want to go under that water, to put his head there. It was too rank. Besides, he couldn't see; the water was dark and dirty. Oh! He pulled and pulled. Not a bit did it give way. This young man had to dive, there, underwater. He went there and he dug there. He pulled out all the roots. The entire plant. Everything. "Is that how you want it?"

"Yes, indeed, that's the way I want it. You'll bring everything, the entire plant. Everything."

And so he came along, the young man. He smelled himself. He stank. Oh, it was awful. And soon afterwards he got sick. He handed the plant to the bear-walker. And he took it.

"Well? Did you learn anything, Anishinaubae?"

"Yeah, I learned that you really wanted this plant is what I learned!"

"Try to remember! Try to remember! Think! Why did you do what you did?"

They went on their way. Now the young man was anxious. Rather than carry on, he quit. It was preferable. "He is much too slow, this one teaching me," the young man decided. He left.

Much later, once, when he was sitting at home there in the big city—it was already winter, and he was sitting. "That's it!" he says. "That's what the bear-walker tried to teach me! If you were to help your fellow Anishinaubaek, or your fellow human beings generally, what you must do is already set. However you may hate it, however unpleasant it may be, you must work at it. It is not always beautiful. And this—everything on the surface of the water is beautiful. To get to the source of beauty you must dig deep."

It has now been seven years since the young man told me that story. It must now be ten years since that happened to him.

This is a relatively new story.

The Great Lynx

Mishi-bizheu

Told by Sam Ozawamik

Collected and translated from the Anishinaubae
by Basil H. Johnston

According to legend, an old man once went to look for his horses. They say that he heard someone cry. A voice was heard calling. This voice was very shrill; it was a powerful voice. Whose it was, no one knew.

The old man went to where the cries were coming from. The woods crossed there. With the cries, he grew afraid. Somewhere in the distance, something was tramping, causing the ground to shake. That is why he fled hard. The old man ran away from there. He ran until he came to a place somewhere near here.

It is said that he was considerably afraid. It was only later that night that he regained his composure. Then he heard a voice calling to him: "Don't ever come again to wherever you hear me. Stay away!"

Somewhat later, he dreamed about this being. In his dream he saw that it was stained black. He saw that its fur was very long and very shaggy. Again it warned him: "Stay away!"

It was in fact the Great Lynx that the old man saw in his dream.

Mer-Man

Nebaunaubae

Told by Basil H. Johnston

Translated from the Anishinaubae
by Basil H. Johnston

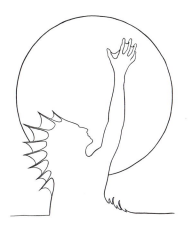

Two Anishinaubaek were travelling inland. In time, one said to the other, "Watch along the way for some place where there is water. At our camp tonight we will need water for cooking."

Sure enough, along the way they located a springwater well. No need to go further; they made camp. When one of them went to fetch water, they say that he saw a fish there, an immense fish, in fact. It was convenient so he scooped him out, took him back to camp.

"Look," he called to his friend, "I bring a fish, I saw him there in the spring."

"You really shouldn't eat that," his friend suggested firmly.

"Don't worry," said the man. "This is a fish, for sure. There is nothing wrong with this fish. Moreover, the water over there flows well."

But even though he cautioned his friend, it was of no use. In spite of the warnings, the Anishinaubae cooked the fish and ate it. His friend didn't.

Later, they lay down to sleep. But the man who had eaten that fish was troubled by thirst. "Am I ever thirsty," he was reported to have said. "Ah! Get me some water."

As requested, his friend fetched him some water, in a dipper. But his thirst was not quenched.

"I pray you," he implored, "get me some more water."

Again the man fetched water for his friend

But even that did not satisfy him. After he requested water a third time his friend lost patience. "That's it!" he snapped. "I tried to advise you against eating the fish. But you would not listen, and this now is the result."

Nevertheless, to please his thirsty friend the man drew more water from the well. This time he set a pail before him. "Here's the water!" he said. "Drink!"

But soon the man drank all of that too.

His friend was furious. "That's it," he said. "I'm not getting water for you again. You would do better to stick your head into the well."

With that, the man left, again to try to quench his thirst. He did not return. He had vanished into the night, that man. His friend could not sleep, not in the least. The night was now very near daylight. Finally, the man went in search of his friend.

When he came to the pool he saw him, but he was already half fish. "It's over," said the mer-man. "It would be better for you to run away. Do not linger too close. Leave. Go to higher ground. Go home. Tell my woman. Some day in the future come here to fish. There are many fish in here."

More water flowed up from that spring and the pool began to spill over. Its water began to flow.

When the mer-man finished speaking his friend hurried to higher land. When he reached the top of a hill he looked down. The well began to flow as a river. Trees were uprooted and tumbled over. Soon a great lake lay below him. How vast it was.

So it's said that through the entire lake there were fish. Such is an Anishinaubae story—wherever there is a lake there will also be fish.

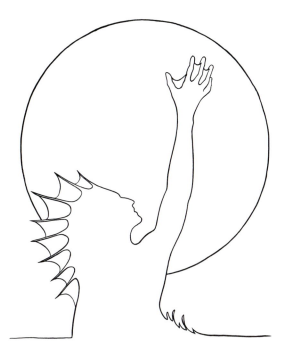

Fish

Geegoohnuk

Told by Sam Ozawamik

Collected and translated from the Anishinaubae
by Basil H. Johnston

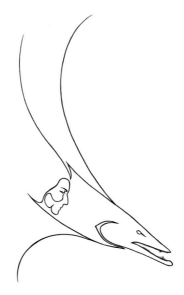

Last winter I heard an old woman telling a story over at Anderson Lake. She spoke English so that the English would understand her.

There was apparently an old man who lived alone in a remote place. He adopted a certain little boy so that the boy would become something. He brought him up well.

One day, when the boy had grown into young manhood, he said to his foster father: "I should look for a woman, a wife."

"I have already chosen one for you," said the old man. "She lives across the water, at the far end of that island. You are old enough now to look for a wife. Then, when I die, you will not be alone, you will not be lonely. There is a canoe—take it. For your journey I will give you a lunch as you leave. Go there directly. Don't stop anywhere, no matter what the reason.

Next day, the young man was on his way. Before he left, however, the old man made him a lunch. When he arrived at the shore he saw that there was a log house to one side of the trail. When they saw him, two young women came out of it.

"Please do come and visit us," they said.

"No, I mustn't," he replied. "I'm going over there."

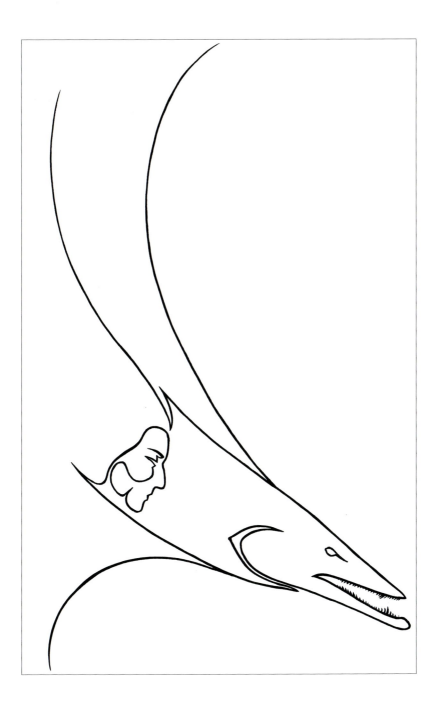

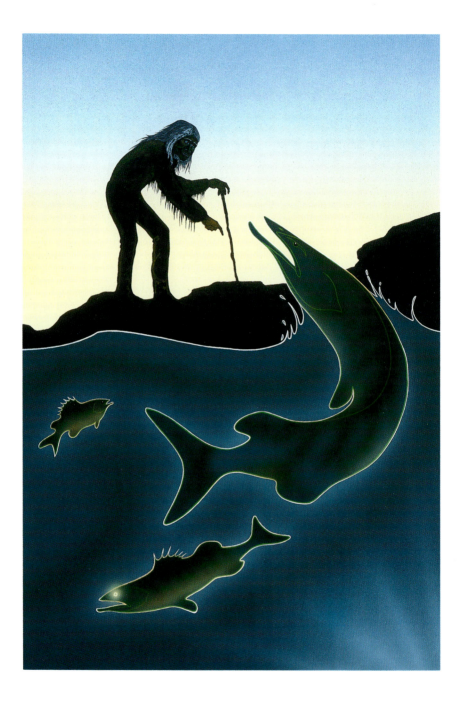

"Oh, don't worry," they said. "She will wait for you. Visit with us. We will feed you."

It is said that while he was eating, the young women's mother came home. My, she was angry, they say. First she bawled out her daughters, then she picked up a club and bludgeoned that young Anishinaubae.

Afterwards, she dragged his body into the water.

The old man waited on and on, they say. Yet there was not the slightest sign of his son. Then he went in search of him. When he found the young man's boat, he immediately knew what had happened. Because of this he prayed.

The next moment, it is said, a fish stuck his head out of the water.

"Get those bones," the old man said to the fish, "and I will give a name to each of you."

Going in all directions, the fish swam away. A short while later (and no more) a fish stuck his head out of the water, a bone in his mouth. Then another, and another. As he had promised, the old man gave a name to each fish as he appeared. By such means, it is said, he was able to collect all the bones, assembling them according to their articulation. Now just what he did is untold; whatever it was, the young man revived.

That is how the fish got their names.

Red Willows

Zeesigoobimeeshuk

Told by Frank Shawbedees

Collected and translated from the Anishinaubae
by Basil H. Johnston

Nanabush was wandering in the far north. He was hungry. Nanabush was always hungry.

He was with his mother at the time. That old lady is known by many names. Some call her "Dodomum" or "Dodum"; others call her "Gushiwun" or "Gushih."

They wandered until Nanabush chanced to meet a bear. "Ha!" he announced. "I'm going to eat you!"

"Oh no you don't," replied the bear. "I will fight back if you try to kill me. Get out of here, Nanabush."

Nanabush would not leave. "Listen," he pleaded, "I'm hungry. Can't you see that? I'm hungry. I've eaten next to nothing for about three days. Maybe four days! I'm going to kill you."

They started fighting somewhere over there, somewhere around Kenora. They battled tooth and nail. They fought in a number of different places along the way, even where Sault Ste. Marie now stands. At the rapids. That really happened. That was all land then. At that time there was no channel of water flowing there.

First, Nanabush would hit the bear; then the bear would hit Nanabush. One time, Nanabush threw the bear so hard against the ground he broke the earth, and the water began to flow through.

That in fact is the reason the water now flows past Sault Ste. Marie.

Finally, Nanabush said to his mother, "You go on ahead and stay there. When I get there too, I will kill this bear." As soon as the word was given, she was gone.

She could hear them battling in the distance. At one point, the bear sent Nanabush flying with such force that he landed on his mother, causing her to fall backwards onto her rump. That is why the lake there is now called "The Old Lady Sat Down."

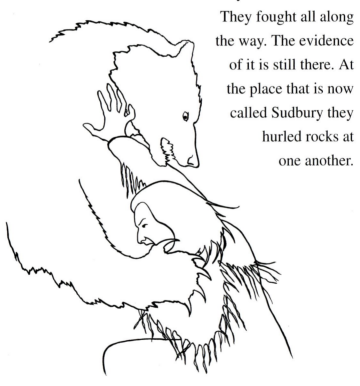

They fought all along the way. The evidence of it is still there. At the place that is now called Sudbury they hurled rocks at one another.

Where they pulled boulders up from the earth, ore was later found. Where they dragged each other along the ground, depressions were made in the land.

Eventually, Nanabush killed the bear, in the general vicinity of Parry Sound.

Meanwhile, his mother came along behind, carrying supplies. She made a fire and put a pot of water over it. Nanabush butchered the bear. When it was cooked, he ate and ate. But he ate too much and very soon suffered from the runs.

"Oh!" He ran over there. "Ah!" Such discomfort. He could not stop going to the toilet. When he sat down to defecate, blood also flowed. He couldn't find anything to use to wipe himself, so he grabbed a sapling and used that. Then he stuck the sapling—with the blood and feces on it—into the earth, somewhere near Parry Sound.

A red willow grew at that spot. Its colour came from the blood of Nanabush.

That is how the red willows came to be.

The Snake and the Man

Ginaebig, Ininih gayae

Told by Frank Shawbedees

Collected and translated from the Anishinaubae
by Basil H. Johnston

Maybe I ought to talk about this one Anishinaubae—all of them in fact, his wife and his children.

Nothing grew very well that summer. As things were, it was already well into autumn, it was hard. They knew that if they got nothing to eat soon they would be eating raw birch. In fact, they might not even see the next summer.

For this reason, the Anishinaubae told his wife: "I have no choice but to go hunting, to look for something for us to eat this coming winter. So long as I kill just one, a moose or even a deer, we would have enough meat for the entire winter. My mind's made up; I will go hunting."

So saying, he took up his bow and was immediately on his way. Oh, he walked for a long time. For a whole day there was nothing; he found nothing. First, he had to kill a squirrel in order to eat, and here and there and from time to time he found wild onions. In this way he had just enough to eat. For a while he walked almost for nothing, looking for trails, hunting. Two days passed, then three. He walks through and near the forest. Ah . . . he walks with purpose, but for nothing. Now he hears something in the distance. He hears something for certain. He hears someone.

"Help me! Help me!"

Oh yes! He listened, but where the sound came from was hard to say. Ah! It's coming from that direction, from the direction where the sun hung, toward the west. That's where the sound was coming from, something calling out to be helped. So, off he went in that direction. On and on he walked. Eventually, he arrives over there where it's clear in the bush. He listens. "It's true," he says, "it comes from over there."

This is what he did next; he went along the edges of the bush. He didn't cut across the clearing. He listens! The sound is much louder.

"Help me! Help me!"

At last he had found the place. It was very thick and bushy. He saw a snake trapped in there. It was the snake himself speaking: "Help me! Help me! I'm stuck! I'm caught!"

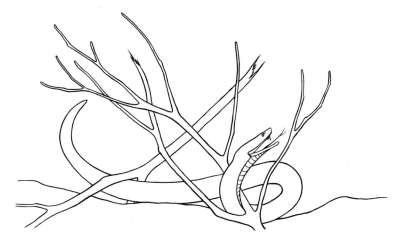

The Anishinaubae spoke to him: "Ah! If I help you, you will kill me."

"Oh, no!" replied the snake. "I would not kill you."

"Are you telling the truth?"

"Yes. Of course I'm telling the truth."

"In that case," said the Anishinaubae, "I'll help you."

Thus assured, he untied the snake. But as soon as the snake was free he instantly tried to kill the Anishinaubae. "Have you forgotten?" screamed the Anishinaubae.

By chance, there was a fox sitting in the forest.

"What in the world is going on over there?" he thought to himself. He went directly near to where they were, even though he knew there might be some danger to him. "They must be reckless," the little fox concluded. "They might even bite my tail, those."

He peeked into where they were fighting un-mercifully.

"Help me! Help me!" the Anishinaubae cried out. "Hurry! The snake is killing me."

The snake himself looked at the man. "Yes, it's true," he commented. "I am going to kill you. But first I'm going to squeeze the life out of you."

The snake squeezed and squeezed, more and more. "Now you can no longer move," he said to the Anishinaubae.

It was at this point that the little fox interrupted them. "What are you doing?" he asked. The Anishinaubae spoke first. "He's fighting me. I helped him there where he was trapped. I freed him there in the thick underbrush. 'I will not kill you,' he promised me. Hardly!"

The fox then turned to the snake. "You, snake. I want to ask you something."

"What is it?" replied the snake.

"Where was it that you were caught? There is no good reason why anyone should get stuck there," said the fox.

"Well, I was stuck there."

"And this Anishinaubae helped you?"

"Yes, indeed!"

"And this is how you repay him?"

"Certainly!"

"I don't believe you," said the fox. "If you in fact were, show me how you were stuck. There is no way anyone could get caught in that place."

The snake was angry. "Alright, then," he said.

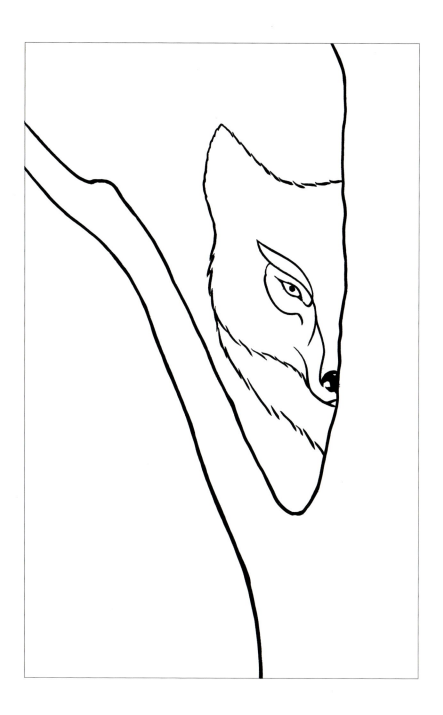

"I will prove my point."

With that, he let go of the Anishinaubae and began crawling across the ground. "This is what I was doing," he announced. Soon enough, he was caught once more.

"Help me! Help me!" he cried out.

The little fox looked at the Anishinaubae. "There now! Be on your way home. Go that way. Go home in a southerly direction; go in a round-about way. After you have travelled for three days, you will come upon a deer."

"How can I thank you?" asked the Anishinaubae.

"Well," said the fox, "in winter we are very hungry while we are going about. Now if it happens that you have something left over, and you throw it outside so that we may eat it, that would be quite enough."

"Agreed," said the Anishinaubae.

The snake was still entangled. He no longer really knew what was going on. He may perhaps even be caught there still. It is quite unlikely that anyone has released him. Just as likely, there may only be bones there. But the snake is already forgotten.

The little fox went along on his way. The Anishinaubae likewise left, and he went in a southerly direction. True enough, he eventually encountered a deer. Using a bow and arrow, he killed the deer.

Then he took it home, cut it up, and stored it away. With that, his family had enough to last them for the entire winter.

The fact was, it already was winter. Very soon it got stormier and stormier. As for the Anishinaubae's wife and children, they didn't have to go looking for what they needed to eat. They had exactly the right amount.

On one occasion, his wife went outside. When she came back in she announced that meat was being stolen from them. "We are being robbed! There's a fox out there! He's stealing meat from us!"

The Anishinaubae grabbed his bow and went out. It was true. There was a fox out there, eating that meat. Without hesitating, he strung his bow and shot that fox. He realized too late what it was he had promised.

The fox was dying. He could only look at the Anishinaubae. "How could you forget?" was the last thing that he said.

The Woodpecker

Paupaussae

Told by Basil H. Johnston

Collected and translated from the Anishinaubae
by Basil H. Johnston

Nanabush did not have an easy time. He was ever hungry. Always, and that's fact, whatever the amount of food available. Once, this Nanabush did something evil. It was probably for this reason that he was condemned to go hungry. When he worked on behalf of his fellow Anishinaubaek, however, he was exceedingly fortunate.

He once came to where an old lady lived. The old lady was making bread when she saw him approaching. "This Nanabush must be hungry," she thought, "and no doubt he has come to beg for food." Not wanting to give any away, she hid these little loaves of bread she had made.

Nanabush walked up to her: "Just in time, couldn't be better," he remarked to the old lady. "You're cooking at this very moment. I'm very hungry. I've eaten nothing for three days. Will you feed me?"

"Oh, alright," she replied. "I'll feed you."

But the old lady was concerned: "I really ought not to feed this Nanabush," she reasoned. "He'll do something to me."

So she cut a very small piece of bread dough and placed it over the fire. Meanwhile, Nanabush went to sleep.

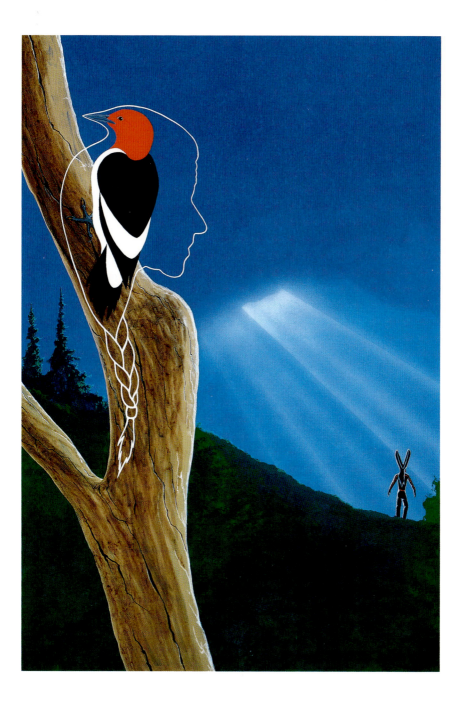

As the dough was heated it swelled to an immense size. Unheard of the length of this bread, or so they say. "I really ought not to give him this bread," she thought. "There's too much of it." So she hid it.

Next, she cut another piece, smaller than the other one. But the same thing happened. That little bit of dough rose and rose. So she hid that one also.

By now there were many loaves of bread lying in a pile. She made sure that all of them were covered and began to bake yet another one.

After a while, Nanabush woke up. "Well!" he remarked. "Have you been baking? Where's all that bread?"

"Oh . . . it's . . . it's not quite ready, not quite yet," she told him, as she placed yet another very small morsel of dough over the fire.

Nanabush immediately knew that he was being deceived by the old woman, so he spoke to her sharply: "If that's the way you want it, okay with me. When I arrived I was very hungry. I asked you to feed me, but you hid those loaves of bread because you are stingy. Fine. From now on you will be a woodpecker. You will have a hard time getting food too, living as you will from a tree."

It is said that in that instant the old woman became a woodpecker.

Bull Frog

Taendae

Told by Sam Ozawamik

Collected and translated from the Anishinaubae
by Basil H. Johnston

This is a story about some young Anishinaubaek, some young Ottawas who were hunting. They were walking near a river—it might have been late evening—and they saw a fire on the other side.

"Let's go there" one of them said. When they crossed the river they saw that the Indians around that fire were not Anishinaubaek. They were probably of the Iroquois tribe. It's said that they were eating.

One of the Anishinaubaek spoke to his partner: "I would very much like to impersonate that bull frog over there. I would like to mimic him."

"Don't! Don't! We will be discovered."

But his friend would not listen, and he began to speak like a bullfrog. One of the Iroquois was gnawing on a bone. He took a long look when he heard this voice. "Not very likely are you a bull frog," he was supposed to have said. Then he threw the bone at the Anishinaubae and hit him dead on.

The two young men noisily churned the water as they tried to flee from there, but they were caught and tied up, perhaps by a rope. The more they struggled to escape, the more their bonds tightened.

The Iroquois led them away, but were these Anishinaubaek ever amused! And did they ever laugh!

They camped that night with their captors.

Next morning, they set out. They were tethered together. At the very least they might have been fed. They continued to laugh heartily.

The Iroquois who was leading the group spoke to another of them:

"Go ask them what they are laughing about, and tell them what is in store for them, where they are being taken." So he asked them, this person who understands. He translated. "What are you laughing at?" he asked them.

"Oh! Him, I'm laughing at my friend who imitated a bull frog, and at what happened to us as a result. I'm laughing at that too."

"Are you not afraid?"

"No," he apparently replied.

As expected, this man reported that, according to what they said, they were not afraid. But the Anishinaubaek thought that they would be killed. Unquestionably. And yet it happened that another was slain, the one who was guarding them. (At night it was almost impossible to keep watch over them.)

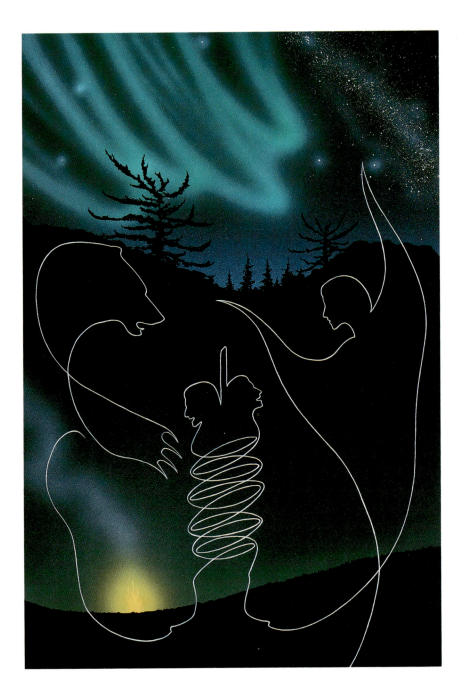

The Anishinaubae asked his friend: "Did you not fast (seek dream)?"

"Yes! Of course! I did fast. How about you?"

"Yes! I did also."

"So! What did you dream?"

"I dreamed of a bear. And you?"

"Oh! A spirit."

In the evening, when the Iroquois were eating their meal, the bear arrived. He severed the ropes. That was it. It was now the shade's turn. Of course a shade is invisible. No one sees him; he is there nevertheless. It was his turn; he summoned the shade. They made their way directly where the others were sitting. Instantly, they disappeared. So they fled.

Apparently, they were sought out, to be fed. But there was no one.

"It is strange," said the Iroquois who was leading. It would be better to leave things be. We cannot sense where they are. It is likely that they glided past us. They must be exceedingly far away by now."

Such, then, is what is said to have happened to the Ottawas. No one could injure an Ottawa. They were very spiritual in ancient times.

Vision

Waussaeyaubindumowin

Told by Sam Ozawamik

Collected and translated from the Anishinaubae
by Basil H. Johnston

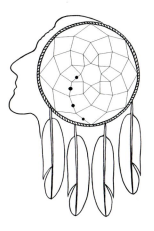

 The Anishinaubaek experienced all sorts of things. I, too, believe the old accounts, as well as the prophecies.

One person prophesied: "It's going to be very difficult," he said. "The order will crumble. Then I will return." Apparently, he decided to leave of his own accord. Something must have happened to him. He died. However, he is to come back again, at some unknown time. It is doubtful, though, whether the Anishinaubaek will believe him.

The man who spoke of this referred to one place before Toronto was there. While there might be some question, it might have existed, just barely. Apparently, one old man described what it was going to look like. And that is what it looks like today.

He said that dwellings would tower into the sky, and he said that there would be vehicles with wheels. Moreover, the trails over which these vehicles were to travel would look like the mesh of a spider's net. Besides, he referred to a trail that led skyward; he was supposed to have said that the trails would be canted this way.

That Anishinaubae was very fanciful. He saw a vision, right here in Little Wikwemikong. The old man was presumably lying down. And he was said

to have been weeping. Then and there he spoke to his father.

"Are you afraid to die?" his father was supposed to have said to him.

"No, I am not afraid to die. Rather, I am weeping because of what is going to happen. Vehicles will run by themselves, and boats will steam under their own power. Many people will lose their lives in the waters. The winds will blow and blow, and water will soar into the air."

That is what one old man said.

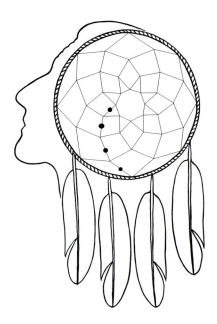